Mathew Brady

Photographer of Our Nation

SHOW ME AMERICA

Mathew Brady

Photographer of Our Nation

Stuart A. P. Murray

Sharpe Focus
an imprint of M.E. Sharpe, Inc.

SERIES CONSULTANT

Jeffrey W. Allison
Paul Mellon Collection
Educator, Virginia Museum of Fine Arts

Cover Photos:
"Portrait of Abraham Lincoln before delivering his Cooper Union address" (Mathew Brady);
"Mathew B. Brady with a battery before Petersburg, VA" (photographer unknown).

Sharpe Focus
An imprint of M.E. Sharpe, Inc.
80 Business Park Drive
Armonk, NY 10504
www.sharpe-focus.com

Copyright © 2009 by M.E. Sharpe, Inc.

Series created by Kid Graphica, LLC
Series designed by Gilda Hannah

Map: Mapping Specialists Limited

Library of Congress Cataloging-in-Publication Data

Murray, Stuart, 1948–
    Mathew Brady: photographer of our nation/Stuart A.P. Murray.
        p. cm. — (Show me America)
    Includes bibliographical references and index.
    ISBN 978-0-7656-8151-5 (hardcover: alk. paper)
    1. Brady, Mathew B., 1823 (ca.)–1896—Juvenile literature. 2. Photographers—
United States—Biography—Juvenile literature. 3. Portrait photography—United
States—History—Juvenile literature. 4. United States —History—Civil War,
1861–1865—Photography—Juvenile literature. I. Title.

TR140.B7M97 2008
779.092—dc22   2008000113

Printed in Malaysia

9 8 7 6 5 4 3 2 1

Contents

Brady, the Grand Old Man of American Photography

Like a ray of light still traveling toward the vision from some past world or star, Mathew B. Brady is at the camera still and if he lives eight years longer will reach the twentieth century and the age of seventy-five. . . . [H]e turned my head a few weeks ago between his fingers and thumb, still intent upon that which gave him his greatest credit—finding the expression of the inner spirit of a man. [Brady's fingers] had lifted the chins and smoothed the hairs of virgin sitters, now grandmothers, the elite of the beauty of their time, and [of] the rulers of parties, sects, agitations and the stage. . . . Brady has been an idealist [and] because he had a higher passion than money, we possess many a face in the pencil of the sun. . . . Brady is not rich. He allowed the glory of the civil war to take away the savings and investments of the most successful career in American photography.

George A. Townsend
New York *World,* April 10, 1891

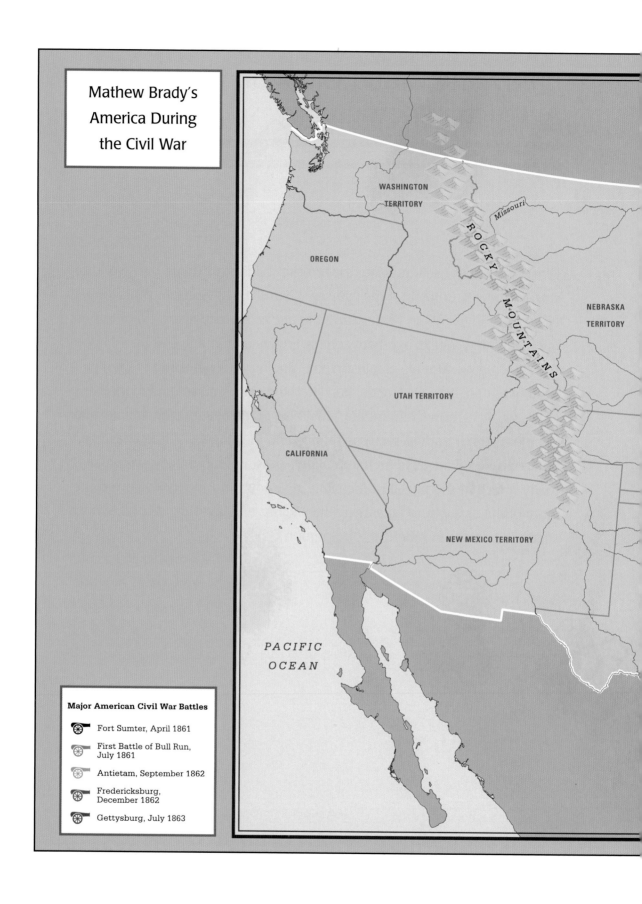

Mathew Brady's
America During
the Civil War

WASHINGTON
TERRITORY

Missouri

ROCKY MOUNTAINS

OREGON

NEBRASKA
TERRITORY

UTAH TERRITORY

CALIFORNIA

NEW MEXICO TERRITORY

PACIFIC
OCEAN

Major American Civil War Battles

Fort Sumter, April 1861

First Battle of Bull Run,
July 1861

Antietam, September 1862

Fredericksburg,
December 1862

Gettysburg, July 1863

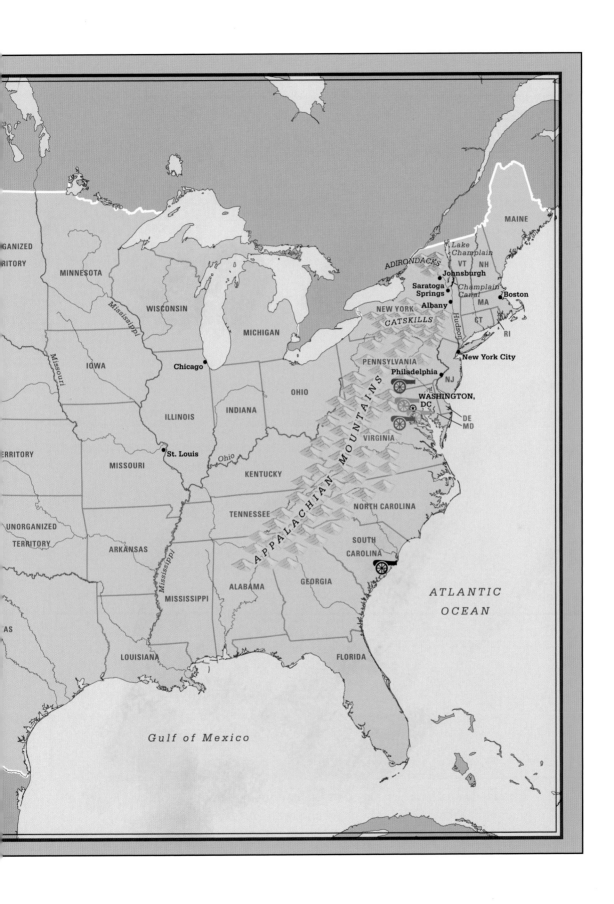

Map   9

The elderly Mathew ß. ßrady was the nation's most famous photographer in 1889, when his nephew and protégé, Levin C. Handy, took this three-quarter-length portrait in their New York City studio.

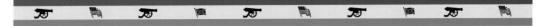

CHAPTER ONE

At the Camera Still

Brady is at the camera still, [continuing] the most
successful career in American photography.
—*George A. Townsend, New York* World *reporter*

I n the spring of 1891, a newspaper reporter who happened to be passing by the gallery of Mathew B. Brady in Washington, D.C., decided to pay the famous photographer a visit. The reporter was amazed by what he found there, and he wrote about his experience in the New York *World*.

"Brady the photographer alive?" he began. "The man who [photographed] Mrs. Alexander Hamilton and Mrs. Madison, Gen. Jackson, and Edgar A. Poe? Thought he was dead many a year.... Brady is at the camera still, [continuing] the most successful career in American photography."

That career, however, had lost its glory. Mathew Brady could no longer afford a handsome studio, nor did he have the funds needed to record events with his camera. Brady already had recorded one of the most important events in the history of the United States—the Civil War of 1861–1865. In doing so, he had spent almost everything he had, and his efforts to assemble thousands of images of the war had ruined him financially. Despite his losses, Brady believed in the importance of his achievements, as he said, "I regarded myself as under an obligation to my country."

Brady's Washington gallery was impressive. On the walls hung hundreds of photographs of public people who lived from the 1830s to the 1890s. There were presidents, queens, and princes; famous generals, politicians, writers, and legendary individuals from America's Revolutionary period. In Brady's successful years, the

"Wounded soldiers being tended in the field after the battle of Chancellorsville near Fredericksburg, Va." Mathew B. Brady, 1863

Federal soldiers survey their dead on the battlefield at Chancellorsville, near Fredericksburg, Virginia, 1863. Mathew Brady and several other photographers journeyed to the scene to record the engagement in which a total of 18,000 Union and Confederate soldiers died.

most powerful, rich, and fashionable people—including celebrities in the theater, business, and science—wanted the words "Photographed by Brady" imprinted on the frames of their portraits.

Also, on his Washington gallery walls were photographs of Civil War generals, spies, and ordinary soldiers who had fought on both sides—some seen lying dead on the battlefield. Pictures of military encampments hung alongside photographs showing the building of the Washington Monument and the Brooklyn Bridge.

Not all of these photographs were made by Brady, but he had taught many of the camera operators who took them. In Mathew Brady's gallery, the visual story of the nineteenth-century United States unfolded under his careful guidance. That guidance had come from a man whose eyesight had declined until he was almost blind. Yet he still led the way in that most visual of arts—photography.

Reproductions of these same photographs hung on the walls of many public buildings and thousands of American homes. They appeared in magazines, newspapers, and books about the nation and its people. "My gallery," Brady said, has been used to "illustrate all the publications in the land."

By 1891, Brady was an old man in failing health, but the *World* reporter saw the "white cross of his moustache and goatee" and "felt the spirit in him still."

As the nineteenth century drew to a close, Americans looked back and were grateful that Brady had captured so much of their past in thousands of pictures. In the twentieth century, Mathew B. Brady and his work would become even more important to the United States than during his own lifetime.

During his four and a half years as president (1861–1865), Abraham Lincoln posed a number of times for Mathew Brady. The two men were good friends when this portrait was taken in 1862.

One admirer who collected Brady photographs wrote about how a camera "can freeze a moving moment or an unforgettable face." Old photographs, he said, allow us to "study scenes and faces from the past" so that we think we were there ourselves or feel we know that person. It is, he continued, "as if I could smell the air or hear the voices, feel the wind, the press of a hand."

Those black and white images from Brady's America do more than tell us about people and places and a historical period. They tell us about Mathew Brady. This renowned American photographer left no writing about himself—there is some question as to whether he could even write. What Brady left, instead, were his pictures, showing how he saw his world and its people. His photographs give us a vivid story that words could never tell more clearly or with more power.

This 1860s landscape by artist John Frederick Kensett shows the rugged mountain scenery around Lake George, New York. Mathew Brady said he was "born in the woods" that surrounded the lake.

CHAPTER TWO

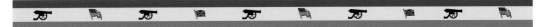

The Pencil of the Sun

I was born in the woods about Lake George
around 1823 or 1824.
—Mathew Brady

When Mathew B. Brady was born in Warren County on the edge of the Adirondack Mountain wilderness in New York State, no local official recorded the time and place of his birth. Brady used to say, "I was born in the woods about Lake George around 1823 or 1824." He never knew the exact year or what the initial "B" stood for.

By 1830, Julia and Andrew Brady and their six children were living in Johnsburgh, a small village near the north branch of the Hudson River in upstate New York. The children were all under ten years of age. Mathew, one of the oldest, was a slender, red-haired boy, shy and quiet. Like the other Brady children, he received little schooling because he had to work to help support the family.

In Johnsburgh, girls helped in the vegetable gardens and around the home. Most of them were married by the time they were sixteen. The boys worked at home, too, until they were old enough to be employed at leather tanneries or sawmills. In the tanneries, they lugged piles of animal hides and mixed vats of the harsh chemicals used in preparing leather. In sawmills, they moved logs or stacked planks and beams.

This kind of hard physical work would be in Mathew's future if he stayed in Johnsburgh. As he grew older, however, he longed to see the wider world, which seemed so distant from the forests and mountains of his home.

By about ten, Mathew had developed an eye infection that caused his eyes to become inflamed. There was no doctor in Johnsburgh who could treat his condi-

Artist John W. Hill portrayed a canal barge drawn by a team of horses through the Erie Canal of upstate New York. Canals were essential American highways for commerce and travel in the nineteenth century.

tion, and besides, his parents couldn't afford it. Then, in 1835, the family saved enough money for a doctor. This meant journeying all the way to Albany, where he would receive medication for his inflammation and a new pair of glasses with stronger lenses.

Down the Hudson

Albany, the capital of New York State, was a long way from Johnsburgh, more than 80 miles (129 kilometers) along the Hudson River. At the time, country people usually walked to get to places. A fortunate traveler might hitch a ride on a slow-moving wagon drawn by horses. Rivers and canals were the best long-distance highways, and towns grew up along them. Johnsburgh and Albany were both on the Hudson, making a boat trip between them much easier than going overland. Even so, eighty miles required several days on the water.

From Johnsburgh, most travelers went by boat down the Hudson to Albany. After leaving the mountains, a passenger might change to a larger boat on the Champlain Canal, which had been built just a few years earlier. The canal was busy with loaded freight boats towed by horses or mules that slowly walked along the shore. Every few miles, there were locks—enclosures where the boats waited for gates to be opened, letting the water out to fill the river's next, lower level. The boats then continued to the next lock. The canal, with locks and gates and machinery, was a fascinating sight for any young man from upcountry.

The Hudson widened as the city of Troy appeared on the left bank. Troy's waterfront was busy and noisy with the thud and clank of machinery. Men shouted and sang as they worked on decks or handled cargo on the wharves. It was here that many travelers from the Adirondacks saw their first steamboat.

EARLY EYEGLASSES

The first practical eyeglasses, also called spectacles, were invented in thirteenth-century Europe but were not common in America until the start of the nineteenth century. Astronomers adapted the magnifying properties of telescope lenses to smaller glass lenses that helped people with reading.

Two famous eighteenth-century Americans who wore eyeglasses were George Washington and Benjamin Franklin. Washington wore glasses specially made by a friend who was also an astronomer. Franklin is said to have designed his own bifocals, meaning lenses divided in two—one part for reading, the other for seeing at a distance.

American opticians steadily improved eyeglasses during the nineteenth century, but it was not until 1841 that another United States president—Andrew Jackson—acquired reading glasses. Even then, however, glasses were seldom worn in public, because they were considered a sign of old age or weakness.

The most popular style of eyeglasses in the mid-nineteenth century had rectangular or egg-shaped frames. These glasses were not very comfortable because they were heavy and had no pads to cushion the bridge of the nose.

Colored glass, usually dark blue, was available for wearers whose eyes were sensitive to strong light. Travelers also wore these early sunglasses to protect their eyes from the bright light streaming through train windows.

The *Clermont,* designed and built in 1807 by Robert Fulton, was the first steamboat to operate on the Hudson River. Officially known as the *North River Steamboat,* it led the way for steam-powered shipping in the United States.

Steamboats came in every size. Some were small, smoke-grimed workboats and towboats, while the largest were handsome white passenger vessels. Flags and pennants fluttered as steamboats sliced through the water. Black clouds spouted from their smokestacks, and paddle wheels churned the river as the chug-chug of mighty engines kept time.

Those engines were driven by the force of steam from huge boilers filled with hot water. Steam moved the engines, which moved mechanical arms on deck that turned the paddle wheels. It was a marvel that steamboats did not need sails or oars or wind.

The world was new, and steam power was the force of the future, but it was not the only invention being talked about. Another was electricity, which scientists were learning to control. And then there was a completely new art, using daylight and chemicals to make a picture appear on a metal plate, as if by magic.

Until this time, artists had made only painted or hand-drawn pictures, but these new images were created without paint or brushes—without an artist's hand! They were pictures made by light, by what was described as the "pencil of the sun." This wider world was exciting, and Mathew Brady wanted to know all about it. First, though, he had to visit the eye doctor in Albany.

A Studio Assistant

Mathew Brady did more than get medicine and eyeglasses on this trip to Albany. He also met William Page, a professional artist about twenty-five years old. Page needed an assistant in his studio and offered Mathew the job. This was a wonderful opportunity for such a young man. Brady moved to Page's home in Saratoga Springs, a resort town north of Albany. In the summertime, many of America's wealthiest people came to Saratoga. Visitors soaked in the famous mineral springs, which were said to cure most ailments. They stayed in fine hotels and enjoyed dancing and dining and watching horse races. They also had artists like Page paint their portraits.

These portraits usually were miniatures painted on porcelain, glass, or ivory, and just a few inches in size. Miniatures could be placed into frames, protective cases, and lockets. Since Brady was skillful with wood and leather, he earned extra money by making cases to hold miniatures.

THE CAMERA OBSCURA

In the tenth century, long before the invention of photography, an Arab scientist, in what is today Iraq, named Abu Ali al-Hasan studied light and its properties, a science known as optics. He invented a device to project an image onto a flat surface, such as a wall or a screen.

Al-Hasan wrote about his experiments in which light entered a dark chamber—a *camera obscura*, in Latin—through a pinhole. This light created a picture on the chamber's far wall, showing an image of the scene outside. Chinese and European scientists studied Abu Ali al-Hasan's experiments and created their own camera obscuras in darkened rooms or tents.

Many artists, including the fifteenth-century Italian Leonardo da Vinci, knew about the camera obscura. Smaller models of the cameras (rooms) were used as drawing aids for artists, who made sketches by tracing the projected images. They then copied their sketches onto canvases and used them to guide their painting. In time, portable cameras were invented, known as "pinhole cameras," which projected images onto paper.

By the eighteenth century, it was common for artists to use camera obscuras, which made their preliminary sketches more accurate and easier to create. By the nineteenth century, a camera could project an image onto a surface treated with light-sensitive chemicals. The result was a photograph, a picture made with light.

With Page as a teacher, Brady's drawing ability improved, and he became an accomplished studio assistant. Page would sketch the portrait of a person—the "subject"—who would sit still for an hour or more to have it done. Next, Brady copied this sketch onto porcelain or glass. Then Page would color Brady's copy to make the finished portrait.

Brady learned how to pose subjects to make them look their best. It was especially important to seat them near a window. Sometimes, he placed a mirror just so, to reflect light onto a subject's face.

In Saratoga, Brady met many wealthy people, and they enjoyed the company of this modest boy from the country with the thick glasses. He admired the "men of achievement," as he called the important individuals he met. It was good work, but he still wanted to know about the new art, the "pencil of the sun."

It turned out that Page had a friend who was experimenting with this art, which was called photography, from the Greek *phos*, for light, and *graphis*, for a drawing tool. That friend, Samuel F.B. Morse, was among the finest painters of the day, and he also was an inventor.

To the Big City

In 1839, Page took Brady to New York City to meet Morse. New York was a bustling, fast-growing seaport. Docks and wharves bristled with the masts of ships. Hurrying people crowded the cobblestone streets alongside horse-drawn wagons, carriages, and carts. New York's population of 300,000 seemed to converge on Broadway, the main avenue.

Morse was well known in the city, teaching art at the University of New York and painting portraits. But most of all, he was an inventor. When Brady and Page entered Morse's studio, they found themselves surrounded by inventions. Thin copper wire stretched back and forth on overhead reels, and tools were everywhere, as were jars and cans of chemicals, paints, oil, canvases, and artists' brushes.

On one table sat a metal instrument attached to the stretched copper wire. This instrument was Morse's electric telegraph key, which sent messages along the wire. Morse hoped to convince the national government to finance the construction of the first telegraph system.

Here in Morse's studio, Brady found the world's most modern example of progress. But it was not the telegraph that interested him. Instead, his gaze turned to several metal plates with small images on them. These pictures, about the size of miniatures, showed buildings, but no people.

Young Mathew Brady would have recognized this 1840s harbor view by Nicolino Calyo. The painting shows New York City on the left and Brooklyn on the right, separated by the East River.

On another workbench, a wooden box, a foot or so square, had a brass lens poking out from one side. Brady wanted to know about this box and about the pictures on the plates.

Morse told him the pictures had been made by the "pencil of the sun." As an ambitious and curious young man with artistic talent, Brady wanted to find out everything about these miniatures and how they could be created by sunlight.

The inventor of the early photographic process that bore his name, Louis Daguerre, sold his patent to the government of France in 1839. The government then gave up all rights to daguerreotypy, calling the technique a "free gift to the world."

CHAPTER THREE

The Art and Science of Photography

It looks like fairy work.
—*New York reporter about daguerreotypy*

The box with the lens was called a camera. It had been designed by Morse's French friend, Louis Daguerre, the world's leader in photography.

The camera was lightproof when the lens was capped. When the lens cap was removed, daylight came into the camera, casting a picture of whatever the lens saw. This picture was reflected on a metal plate covered with silver, like a mirror. The silver was coated with chemicals that were light-sensitive, meaning they turned dark when exposed to sunlight. The image was burned onto the chemicals on the metal plate.

This process was named daguerreotypy, after its inventor Louis Daguerre, and the resulting picture was a daguerreotype. Daguerreotypes were beautiful and clear, but very small, about the size of a miniature portrait. Newspapers around the world were talking excitedly about daguerreotypes. One New York reporter said, "It looks like fairy work"—like magic.

Morse and other inventors experimented with chemistry to improve on that magic. They were discovering the best chemicals to use and also developing the camera and lens designs. Morse wanted to shorten the exposure time needed for light coming through the lens, which was then about ten minutes. With such a long exposure time, daguerreotypy could capture a scene that did not move—such as buildings and the countryside. Anything that moved either would not be recorded or would be blurred during a long exposure. If exposure times could be reduced to just a few minutes or less, it would be possible to make pictures of people—as long as the subjects sit perfectly still.

This 1837 still-life image by Louis Daguerre is one of the first daguerreotypes. The inventor of photography was already famous for his diorama exhibitions—large, dramatic landscapes illuminated by reflected daylight that changed in intensity.

This was all fascinating to young Mathew Brady, who stayed in New York to become Morse's pupil. Page soon returned to portrait painting, while Brady took daguerreotype classes in what was the country's first school of photography. Morse was a fine instructor, and he had an excellent student in Brady.

To make a living while he studied with Morse, Brady continued making cases for miniatures. He also worked as a clerk in the department store of A.T. Stewart, one of Manhattan's largest retailers.

LOUIS DAGUERRE, PHOTOGRAPHIC PIONEER

Louis-Jacques-Mandé Daguerre, the French inventor of the first practical process of photography, was also an artist, like Morse. Daguerre had been a scene painter for opera sets in the 1820s when he began experimenting with light and light-sensitive chemicals.

In 1829, in his early forties, Daguerre formed a partnership with inventor Joseph Niépce (pronounced Nee-ps) to improve a new photographic process. Although Niépce died in 1833, Daguerre would share all profits from the patent of this new process with his partner's surviving family members.

Daguerre finally invented the world's most effective method of photography, which he named the daguerreotype. In 1839, he sold the rights for the process to the French government, making it public for the first time. Soon, daguerreotypists around the world were studying this Frenchman's new process, and the age of photography was born.

In 1826, French chemist and physicist Joseph Niépce produced the world's first photograph on metal. Niépce later worked with Louis Daguerre to improve the process, which was named daguerreotypy.

Small cases had been used for centuries to hold miniature portraits. Usually, the case was of wood, covered with leather or cloth. It was held together with metal fasteners and had a hinge for opening and closing the lid.

The portrait sat snugly in the back of the case, which the owner could open to look at the picture. The most common case was rectangular, but fancier styles could be worn on necklaces as lockets, and others were pinned to a garment or even attached to a ring.

Brady also made miniature cases to hold jewelry, and this became another profitable career. Before he was a famous daguerreotypist, Mathew Brady was known as "a jewel case man."

Untitled. Mathew B. Brady. c 1850

This original Mathew Brady daguerreotype, held in a jewel case made by Brady, belonged to a prosperous Philadelphia family. The embossed address on the interior of the case reads "Brady & Gallery—206 & 207—Broadway, New York," the address of his studio between 1844 and 1853.

A Palace for the Sun

Over the next few years, Brady was often in a laboratory Morse used at the university. Here, a large glass room had been built on the rooftop. This "palace for the sun," as the inventors called it, directed sunlight into Morse's studio, making it easier to experiment with cameras, chemicals, and daguerreotypes.

In the studio, large mirrors were placed at angles to reflect light. Window shades could be pulled down to soften bright daylight or opened to increase the light. The experimenter recorded work in daily journals, noting exposure times used for certain light and weather conditions: sunny, cloudy, clear, foggy, dry, or humid. Different light and atmospheric conditions required different exposure times, depending on which chemicals were used. Morse and other daguerreotype experimenters improved the process until exposure times were less than a minute—short enough to photograph a human face.

The position of the sun also determined the amount and strength of light available in the studio. The most intense light was when the sun was overhead at noon. In the morning and late afternoon it was low in the sky, so its light was not as strong.

Although Brady had received little formal education, he learned the art and science of daguerreotypy from Morse and the other inventors, who were equally brilliant. In fact, the finest scientist working to develop daguerreotypes and their chemicals was Dr. John W. Draper, head of the university's chemistry department. Draper had studied sunlight for many years and was a specialist in the effect of light on certain chemicals. He brought extensive knowledge to his partnership with Morse.

Morse continued developing his telegraph and trying to convince the government in Washington, D.C., to back him financially. Meanwhile, he was beginning to take daguerreotype portraits for a fee.

The Daguerreotype Business

Many New Yorkers and visitors to the city had heard about daguerreotype portraits and wanted them for themselves. After a number of other young men took lessons from Morse, commercial "daguerreotype galleries" began springing up. No other city in the world had as many daguerreotype studios—more than 900 by 1845!

Daguerreotype likenesses were just 1 or 2 inches wide and tall, much like the miniature portraits artists painted on porcelain, glass, or ivory. Like these miniatures, the "pencil-of-the-sun" pictures were fragile and could be easily scratched. They were best protected by a case—a Mathew Brady case.

In 1843, the government at last commissioned Morse to build the first long-distance telegraph line, which stretched between Washington, D.C., and Baltimore. The inventor threw himself fully into this work and withdrew from daguerreotypy.

The following year, Brady went into business for himself. He left Stewart's department store and opened his own portrait studio, calling it Brady's Daguerrean Miniature Gallery. He was just twenty-one years old.

This portrait of Mathew Brady shows him in 1861, at the start
of the American Civil War and at the height of his career.

CHAPTER FOUR

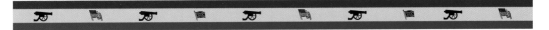

Brady's of Broadway

The grouping together of the most distinguished men of
the Nation into a Gallery like this, and at a period like
this, is not only a noble and patriotic design, but it will
furnish a moment of art and patriotism for coming times.
—New York reporter

Brady's first place of business was on the corner of Fulton Street and Broadway. From the start, he had plenty of competition, since many other daguerreotype galleries were clustered close by. People who wanted to have their likenesses taken had a wide range of choices.

Every other large American town had daguerreotype galleries, with the best being in Boston, Philadelphia, Washington, D.C., and Chicago. Daguerreotype portraits became all the rage. While only the wealthiest people could afford to have portraits painted, a daguerreotype likeness was affordable, and it could be taken and framed in just a few hours.

Good light was essential to making a daguerreotype, so Brady chose the top floor for his studio. Carpenters built skylights in the roof to let in more daylight. Brady was one of the first daguerreotypists to understand the importance of skylights as part of his photographic equipment.

Brady's experience in Page's Saratoga portrait studio was valuable. There he had learned procedures used for centuries in portrait studios. These included how to position the sitter so that daylight illuminated the person's face, eliminating shadows.

Studio light was even more important to daguerreotype artists than to painters. While a painter could add light-colored paint wherever desired in a portrait, the daguerreotypist's camera recorded what was in front of it. If a face was in shadow or

Mathew Brady was not the only proprietor of an elegant photography studio. Greek statuary and handsome furniture are prominent in this 1854 lithograph of Ball's Daguerrean Gallery of the West in Cincinnati, Ohio.

the light was too bright, the resulting daguerreotype would be unsatisfactory. Sittings were done in the middle of the day, for the best light. When it was cloudy, no pictures could be taken, and appointments were cancelled.

Brady developed techniques that made a picture clearer. Too often, daguerreotype portraits had spots of glare or dark shadows. Brady worked to avoid such problems. He made sure to cover white clothing during part of an exposure to prevent glare. He also reflected light into dark features, such as eyes, and applied makeup to his subjects as needed. Sometimes he made sunken cheeks look fuller by placing wads of cotton in the person's mouth.

It was also important that the daguerreotype artist make the subject relax. A nervous or unhappy subject would look stiff or grumpy. The resulting portrait would not please anyone. The artist had to make the subject feel comfortable, sometimes by joking a bit.

A relaxed subject in a good mood made for a more pleasing picture. Brady's knowledge of posing subjects set him apart from other daguerreotypists. So, too, did his experience dealing with Saratoga tourists.

Although he had been born a poor country boy, Brady had worked with the wealthiest of clients in Page's studio. Having rich clients in New York City meant he could charge more for his work and so take more time for a sitting.

Some fast daguerreotype operators had as many as twenty sittings a day and charged just 25¢ for a picture. The results, however, were usually inferior pictures. Brady scheduled only six sittings daily, and his daguerreotypes cost $3 to $5 each.

A PICTURE BY BRADY

In the mid-nineteenth century, New York was one of the world's busiest and richest cities. Yet it also had thousands of poor people, crowded into tumble-down buildings and crime-filled neighborhoods. These areas had names such as "Hell's Kitchen" and "Poverty Flat."

The city was growing fast. Great numbers of people came from abroad and from the American countryside to find work. Street stalls sold everything from clothing to beer. The city's many workshops rang with the sound of hammers and the squeal of pulleys, while steam-powered machines rumbled in the larger factories. Still, most 1840s residents could find only jobs that paid pennies a day. Some did much better, making a dollar a day, a very good wage at that time.

It was remarkable that the daguerreotypy rage was so catching—even among poorer people. Almost everyone saved their pennies to have a picture taken. New York author Bret Harte wrote a verse about struggling New Yorkers determined to have a daguerreotype portrait—especially one colored by an artist:

> *If you saw papa's picture, as taken*
> *By Brady, and tinted and that,*
> *You'd never suspect he sold bacon*
> *And flour at Poverty Flat.*

Brady's customers were willing to pay such a high price because the quality of his portraits was so much better.

As he posed his clients, Brady moved efficiently about the studio, always charming and well-dressed in the latest style. While chatting with the subject, he made sure the camera's images were technically excellent and sharply focused. Only when the light was perfect and the sitter looked natural was the picture taken. As his business grew, Brady hired camera operators and taught them to take pictures after he had posed the subjects.

Particularly important portraits were touched up by a skilled studio artist—often by Brady himself. He sometimes treated porcelain and ivory with photographic chemicals and made daguerreotypes directly on this material. A portrait also could be hand-colored, and the result was somewhat like a painted miniature.

Portraits often were framed and hung in the studio's gallery or displayed in glass cases. Customers could look at the pictures on display and choose how they would like their own picture to be posed and framed.

"Edwin Forrest." Mathew B. Brady, 1842

Shakespearean performer Edwin Forrest was the most famous American actor of the day when Brady made this collodion negative portrait of him. Brady photographed Forrest many times over the years.

There was something special about Brady's ability to capture the sitters' personalities and bring out their best. Photography did, indeed, require artistic skills, and many daguerreotypes were outstanding works of art. The young Mathew Brady earned a reputation as the country's finest daguerreotype portrait artist.

A Famous Clientele

Brady's gallery business boomed along with the rapid growth of both daguerreotypy and New York City. During his first year in business, he won a citywide daguerreotypy competition. The resulting publicity helped his studio become well-known as "Brady's of Broadway."

Because of this growing reputation, a number of famous people came to Brady for their portraits. These included world-renowned Swedish singer Jenny Lind, as well as actors, authors, foreign diplomats, businessmen, military officers, and state governors.

Some clients even linked the gallery to colonial times: Brady photographed former First Lady Dolley Madison as well as the wife of founding father Alexander Hamilton. He also hired a camera operator to take the portrait of the elderly and frail former president Andrew Jackson at his home in Tennessee.

Brady now resolved to collect portraits of as many famous individuals as possible. In some cases, he made daguerreotype copies of portraits taken by others. When he did this, he credited himself as the photographer—a common practice in this time. A daguerreotype could be copied by taking a new daguerreotype of the original one. There was no other way to reproduce an image. One of the most famous of Brady's copies was of former president John Quincy Adams.

In the future, after collecting thousands of images, Brady would not remember which he had taken and which were by other photographers. Almost everything was labeled "By Brady."

One day, the poet and writer Edgar Allan Poe came to the studio with a friend who wanted a portrait. A Poe admirer, Brady was eager to add him to the collection. He offered to take the writer's picture, but Poe declined. Realizing Poe probably could not afford to pay, Brady asked to have the honor of photographing him for no charge. Poe agreed. Brady later made a number of copies, which he sold to poets and other admirers of Poe. "Many a poet has had that daguerreotype copied by me," Brady later recalled.

Brady collaborated with other leaders in daguerreotypy and consulted with chemists and artists. When the day's customers had left, he spent time trying different chemicals, lenses, and exposures. He continued learning from scientists who studied the lat-

This portrait of author and poet Edgar Allan Poe was in Brady's collection of famous individuals. Although this particular image is a copy of another photographer's work, Brady personally knew Poe, who also sat for him.

No celebrity in Brady's time was more famous, or more beloved, than Jenny Lind, the "Swedish Nightingale." Every photographer hoped to have her pose for him when she visited New York in the 1850s, but a mutual friend persuaded Lind to sit for Brady.

"John Q. Adams." Mathew B. Brady, c. 1860

Brady collected photographs by others, copied and reproduced them, and offered prints for sale. It is likely that Brady acquired this portrait of former president John Quincy Adams for his collection.

est combinations of photosensitive chemicals. For example, they taught him to coat the finished picture with enamel, which dried hard and clear and helped protect it from scratching.

Inventors and technicians who made optical lenses for telescopes and microscopes developed lenses for daguerrean cameras. There was also a new magazine dedicated to daguerreotypy, and Brady read it closely to keep up with the latest news. Methods changed with each discovery and improvement in America and Europe.

But over several years, Brady's eyesight became ever weaker, and he began wearing distinctive spectacles with thick blue lenses, which protected his eyes from strong

A MEMORABLE SITTING

Brady's photography sessions did not always go smoothly. In 1864, the newly promoted commander of all Union forces, General Ulysses S. Grant, came to Brady for a portrait. With Grant were impatient government officials who were anxious to get this over with so that the general could leave for the battlefront.

Grant posed, but just as Brady prepared to insert a wet plate into the camera, a cloud covered the sun, darkening the room. The nervous officials fussed when Brady sent a man up to the roof to let in light by removing a shade covering a skylight. Suddenly, the skylight's glass came crashing down, shattering all around the general, and some large pieces barely missed him. The assistant had accidentally stepped through the sky-light—an extremely em-barrassing moment for Brady!

Grant was calm, however, not moving a muscle. Brady took the portrait.

Afterward, an official then pulled Brady aside and pleaded with him not to tell anyone about the incident. It might start rumors that someone had attempted to assassinate the general. Brady and Grant kept this secret for many years.

"Ulysses S. Grant (1822–1885), as an officer." Mathew B. Brady, c. 1864

This 1864 portrait of the Union general Ulysses S. Grant was one of several by Brady, who followed Grant's career throughout the war and Grant's presidency.

Brady photographed several groups of Native American chiefs who came to Washington, D.C., as delegates for their peoples. These Sioux and Arapaho Indians wear their finest formal dress and carry ceremonial pipes.

light. For a professional photographer whose work required good vision, this steady failing of his eyes was a lifelong hardship. Ever-stronger glasses helped Brady fight this condition, which he did with great determination. He depended on camera operators to handle the focusing while he set up the lighting and posed the subject. These two extremely important studio photography tasks were Brady's special skill, and few photographers could compare with him in this area.

Mathew Brady's elegant style of dress and his weak eyes are
evident in this 1860s self-portrait. Although early photography was a complicated and delicate process, the best
studio pictures were exquisitely detailed and perfectly clear.

CHAPTER FIVE

The Best in the World

*A variety of unique and rare photographic
specimens are included in [this] collection,
together with portraits of many of the most
distinguished citizens of the United States.*
—Mathew Brady

Brady was earning considerable profits. He expanded his business to new quarters, where the gallery and waiting areas were more comfortable and better furnished. He hired the best operators and studio assistants, although he remained in charge of the overall work.

The portraits of well-known people on exhibit at the gallery attracted a lot of public interest. Visitors wanted to know what the famous people they had heard and read about actually looked like. Many customers wanted to buy pictures of writers or politicians or actors whom they admired and hang them on their walls at home. Newspapers could include line engravings, or drawings, but printers had not yet discovered how to publish photographs.

Brady made daguerreotype copies of the most popular images and sold them to his customers. Before long, many American homes had a Brady portrait of a president or other celebrity hanging on the walls.

The famous faces on Brady's walls, along with Poe, eventually included almost all the living former presidents, explorer John C. Frémont, artists Thomas Cole and John J. Audubon, circus showman Phineas T. Barnum, and author James Fenimore Cooper. The names of Brady's subjects would fill America's history books, among them poet and journalist William Cullen Bryant, editor Horace Greeley, naval commodore Matthew Perry, and President Zachary Taylor and his cabinet. As he had with Poe, Brady frequently offered famous subjects free sittings as long as he could keep any extra pictures for himself.

ENGRAVING AN IMAGE

In the mid-1800s, printers published a picture by first cutting, or engraving, a copy of it onto special wooden blocks, stone tablets, or metal plates. The engraver copied an image by scratching a series of short lines (small furrows, cuts, or hachure marks) into the surface. This is called line engraving.

Not only did the engraver copy the outlines of a picture's figures, trees, animals, buildings, and so on, but he engraved the shading using small lines. Darker places had more lines, which were closer together, and lighter areas had fewer lines.

These engraved blocks or plates were placed in a wooden form alongside any accompanying type, if this was a magazine or newspaper. Then, the engraving and type were locked onto the printing press. Ink was applied but stayed only on the letters of type and in the cuts of the line engraving. The press printed each sheet of paper by pressing against the inked illustration and type.

When photography became popular, engravers copied a photograph as they would any picture. What was especially exciting was that the photograph was taken originally from life and was not an artist's drawing. The engraver was working from an exact image of the subject, and readers could see what a well-known person actually looked like.

There was no method for printing photographs in the mid-nineteenth century, so pictures were copied by artists who engraved images onto a block of wood that was placed on a printing press. This 1855 engraving of poet Walt Whitman was made from a daguerreotype portrait.

In those days, a subject never smiled for a picture, so the photograph could make a person seem very serious, even grim. One of Brady's grimmest portraits was of Massachusetts statesman Daniel Webster. In reality, Webster was cheerful and joking during the sitting, nothing like the apparently grave and serious man shown in the picture.

Brady chose a dozen of his portraits for a special "Gallery of Illustrious Americans." Included were elderly statesmen Henry Clay, John C. Calhoun, and Webster, as well as Frémont and Presidents Taylor and Jackson. Brady hired an artist to copy and enlarge these portraits. The portraits were engraved onto special stone tablets so that they could be printed as lithographs.

These lithographs were exhibited in the gallery and became a major attraction to visitors, who paid admission to view the collection. Among these statesmen were political opponents, who represented the deepening divide between the North and the South. Kentuckian Clay, for example, was a passionate public speaker in favor of maintaining slavery while keeping the Union together. South Carolina's Calhoun was a firm supporter of the right of states to secede—to leave the Union if they disagreed with national policy. Webster was a New Englander who opposed slavery but worked to reach agreements that would keep the nation from being broken in two because of the issue.

In 1850, the portraits were published in a large-format book along with biographical essays about each individual. One New York journalist who admired Brady's *Gallery of Illustrious Americans* referred to the worsening political troubles between North and South: "The grouping together of the most distinguished men of the Nation into a Gallery like this, and at a period like this, is not only a noble and patriotic design, but it will furnish a moment of art and patriotism for coming times."

Washington City Studio

Although New York had many important people, most leading politicians and diplomats lived in Washington, D.C. It would be a good place for America's most famous daguerreotypist, so Brady opened a temporary studio there in 1847, while still keeping his New York business going.

Washington City, as the nation's capital was called, was raw and muddy, with the Capitol dome still under construction. A large number of well-known people came to Brady's studio, and many became his personal friends. He was even invited to the White House to photograph President James K. Polk, which was done in a dining room.

It was in Washington that Brady met and fell in love with Juliette Handy, a sophis-

Gallery of Illustrious Americans

Former Massachusetts senator Daniel Webster was among the first subjects in Brady's Gallery of Illustrious Americans. Artist Daniel D'Avignon engraved Brady's daguerreotype portraits in order to produce printed copies.

Explorer and California senator John C. Frémont joined Brady's dozen famous men in his Gallery of Illustrious Americans. In 1850, these lithographs were reproduced in an elegant, oversized book that did not sell very well.

ticated Maryland woman. Mathew and Juliette soon married, and she happily shared the life of a photographer. The Bradys' lifestyle included attending fashionable parties and giving their own to entertain friends and clients. Rapidly becoming wealthy, they traveled back and forth between New York and Washington, living in fine hotels. The Bradys never did own a home, but their rooms in these hotels were permanent apartments. They enjoyed the comforts of hotel life and liked having the always-changing company of hotel guests coming and going from around the world.

Creating a Photograph

In 1851, the Bradys sailed to England, where Mathew exhibited forty-eight portraits at the Crystal Palace Exhibition in London. The exhibition sponsored the first-ever international competition for the world's finest photographers, who came from six countries.

All three daguerreotype medals went to Americans, including Brady. One Ameri-

Some of Brady's "Illustrious Americans" were living links to the establishment of the young United States. Statesman Henry Clay was known as the "Western Star" among his colleagues. He died soon after this portrait was taken.

This lithograph of John C. Calhoun completed Brady's collection. Calhoun, Clay, and Webster were famous legislators in the first half of the nineteenth century, but before Brady's collection, their faces were unknown to the public.

can, Dr. John W. Draper, won for a daguerreotype of the moon. This image, taken through a telescope, was so precise that the moon's craters could be clearly seen, as if the viewer were looking through the telescope. After the triumph at the London exhibition, the Bradys traveled around Europe on a journey that lasted ten months. Managers took charge of the gallery in New York, while the Washington gallery was closed. On this trip, Brady acquired pictures from European photographers, images of royalty and famous politicians. He wanted to copy these photographs and add them to his collection of notable people.

In England, Brady studied a new process, known as wet-plate, or collodion, photography. This method involved coating a piece of glass with a light-sensitive chemical mixture called collodion. The coated glass was then placed in the camera, and when the lens was uncovered, the glass received the light. This exposure made a negative, or reverse, image.

Mathew Brady joins his wife, Juliette Handy Brady (left),
and her sister, identified only as Mrs. Haggerty, in 1851.
This is one of Brady's most admired images, studied for its
controlled lighting, its balanced placement of subjects, and
for their natural, rather than stiff, expressions.

Unlike the sheet of metal that received the photographic image in the daguerreotype process, the glass negative was not the final step. Next, it was placed on a sheet of paper that had been specially treated with its own light-sensitive chemicals. Light passed through the glass negative and onto the paper, printing the negative image as a positive—creating a photograph.

While a daguerreotype picture was one of a kind, a glass negative could be used over and over. It could be used to make as many paper prints as the photographer wished. The method was called wet-plate, because the chemicals on the sheet of glass had to be slightly wet, or sticky, when placed in the camera.

Brady knew that this new method was the future of photography, and he began to hire expert cameramen who had mastered the collodion process. One such expert was Alexander Gardner, who reorganized Brady's gallery and laboratories for wet-

This 1840 photograph of the full moon was one of the first ever taken through a telescopic lens. It was made by Brady's colleague Dr. John W. Draper, a New York chemistry professor and early daguerreotypist.

plate photography. Gardner was also a leader in an exciting new method of enlarging photographic prints.

Brady and others continued to make daguerreotype portraits, but the wet-plate method—with glass negatives and prints on paper—soon dominated the fast-changing world of photography. There were more than 3,000 daguerreotype studios in New York at the time. Brady would take the lead among the photographers once again, and they would soon follow him in the wet-plate process.

By 1858, Brady had opened a permanent studio in Washington. That city was bustling more than ever, as Northerners and Southerners argued bitterly over the nation's future.

Alexander Gardner came to America from Scotland to work with Brady in New York and Washington, D.C. This is the earliest known photograph of Gardner, who later set out on his own to become one of the great Civil War battlefield photographers.

Brady's gallery at Tenth and Broadway, opened in 1860, was in the center of New York's booming business district when this engraving was made in January 1861. The illustration was featured in *Leslie's Weekly* newspaper, which often copied Brady photographs of newsworthy individuals and published them as line engravings.

Gardner would run this new National Photographic Art Gallery, as the business was described in Brady's public announcements. Like the New York gallery, it exhibited pictures of famous people. Brady wrote, "A variety of unique and rare photographic specimens are included in [this] collection, together with portraits of many of the most distinguished citizens of the United States."

The Bradys lived in New York for the most part, and Mathew took few photographs in Washington. Still, only Brady's name would be credited on Brady gallery pictures, even when they were taken by Gardner or other staff photographers. Mathew Brady had the status of artist, while the others were operators.

Brady's studio developed a method for touching up pictures. Some originals, like this image of financier and philanthropist George Peabody, were called "Imperial Prints" and were almost two feet tall.

CHAPTER SIX

The Eve of Civil War

Soul-lit shadows now around me;
They who armies nobly led;
They who make a nation's glory
While they're living—when they're dead . . .
—*Caleb Lyon*

One specialty of Brady's was called an imperial photograph. This was an enlarged print, 17 by 20 inches (43 by 51 centimeters) in size. The imperial image was touched up by Brady's staff artists, whose skillful brush strokes made the portrait look more perfect.

The touch-up artist—usually a woman—smoothed out mussed hair and wrinkled clothes. A touch-up masked facial blemishes or brought out highlights in eyes. In some cases, the imperial was completely painted over by an artist, and the result was a color portrait—an expensive one. Brady could get as much as $750 for an imperial finished in oil paints.

Brady liked painting over photographic portraits, because it brought him back to his youthful training as an artist. Often, a subject was photographed against a blank background such as a screen or wall. Then artists would work on the printed picture. They painted in backgrounds: trees, sky, ornamental gardens, or entire landscapes, just as in a formal portrait painting.

The public was delighted and amazed to view these large images, which hung in Brady's gallery. Other photographers began to make their own enlargements, and the galleries competed to print the largest pictures. Eventually, Brady printed on banners, 50 feet (15 meters) tall, and hung them outside his gallery. No one could match those enlargements.

Views of Niagara Falls were popular subjects for landscape painters in the 1850s, when Brady and his crew made this gold-toned daguerreotype. Brady stands third from the right.

Imperials also included pictures from city life, such as street scenes and views of the new Central Park being constructed. Until now, almost all photography had been studio portraits, seldom landscapes. More and more photographers were recording the world around them, as landscape painters did. It was difficult to work with photographic chemicals and negatives outdoors—even in a closed tent—since dust and heat and wind could foul up the developing process. Still, Brady arranged for crews to photograph interesting sites, such as Niagara Falls and New York City's harbor.

Outdoor views often were copied as line engravings for publication by magazines and newspapers. The published images carried the credit, "From a picture by Brady," which further built up the photographer's fame and reputation.

Photographs for Everyone

Photography became ever more appealing to Americans. Another popular new development was the "stereoscopic photograph," which was to be seen through a special viewer—a box with two holes for the spectator's eyes. The stereoscope camera had two lenses and captured two identical images of the same subject. When both images were seen through the viewer, the picture seemed three-dimensional. Before long, many American households had their own stereoscopic viewers and were collecting stereo pictures.

One of the most exciting photographic novelties was the *carte de visite,* which became a passion around the world. This card had a small photograph with the subject's name printed beneath it. The picture, usually 2½ by 4 inches (6 by 10 cm), was used as a "calling card"—the meaning of the French term *carte de visite.* People left their cards behind wherever they visited.

Special cameras were developed with several lenses that could take four or six cartes de visite images at the same time. In this way, orders could be filled rapidly by the gallery. An immensely profitable new business got underway for Brady, with thousands of cartes de visite sold each month. He also collected other photographers' pictures and turned them into cartes de visite.

It suddenly seemed everyone wanted cartes de visite and bought them by the dozen. One reason for such enthusiasm was that Americans were collecting cartes de visite and other photographic portraits and gluing them into picture albums.

The enthusiasm for picture albums opened up other business opportunities for Brady. He arranged to sell copies of his negatives of famous individuals to the country's largest photography supply house, E. and H. T. Anthony and Company of New York. Anthony would sell copies of the images to customers who were making picture albums—an item that Anthony also sold in large numbers. Many American families had several photo albums filled with personal pictures pasted alongside pictures of famous individuals.

The arrangement with Anthony and Company was important to Brady, who traded his negatives for Anthony's photographic supplies. Brady's business was growing fast, and there were many such details to oversee. At times it grew too fast. Although he was wealthy and had invested in valuable city lots and in stocks, Brady did not attend to his business's many financial details very carefully.

Income was high, but bills were too often left unpaid, and proper records were not kept. Even carpenters who worked on remodeling the galleries found themselves having to demand that Brady pay them on time. This was a sign of troubles to come.

CALLING IN PERSON

Life moved slowly in Mathew Brady's world without electronic communications. Contact from a distance was done by cards and letters, often requiring a wait of many days for an answer. The other choice was to visit in person. In many cases, the person being visited was not at home or in the office, so the visitor left a written message, often on a carte de visite. By leaving a carte de visite that had a portrait, the visitor could show what he or she looked like.

Of course, it was necessary to receive a written answer to know when to return. Messenger boys were used when communication had to be immediate. Cities had hundreds of boys dashing to and fro with notes and letters that required immediate replies.

The telegraph system sent instant messages between its offices, but again, messengers had to hurry off and find the person who was to receive the telegram. In 1850, every message was finally carried by a person, whether it was in the form of a telegram or on a carte de visite.

Brady took this photograph of three members of America's best-known antislavery family, probably about 1860. Author Harriet Beecher Stowe wrote the popular 1852 novel, *Uncle Tom's Cabin;* her father, Lyman Beecher, and brother, Henry Ward Beecher, were firebrand preachers and public speakers.

"Harriet Beecher Stowe, Lyman Beecher, and Henry Ward Beecher." Mathew B. Brady, date unknown

"Thomas Jonathan ('Stonewall') Jackson, as a lieutenant during the Mexican War." Mathew B. Brady, 1852

Brady's collection of notable people included this portrait of Mexican War lieutenant Thomas J. Jackson. In the Civil War, Jackson earned the name "Stonewall" as a Confederate general for his heroic action of not retreating when his brigade was under assault.

A Passionate Collector

Mathew Brady's greatest passion was not managing his business, but collecting photographs of famous people. He wanted as many such pictures as he could get, whether he or his staff took them or he bought them from other photographers. Pictures of royalty, stage performers, circus celebrities, politicians, Native American chiefs, and foreign diplomats all found their way into Brady's collection.

In 1860, the Prince of Wales—future King Edward VII of Great Britain—visited New York City, which erupted in excitement, with parades and balls and celebrations. The prince already had heard of Brady's fame and of his award-winning portraits at the 1851 London exhibit. Every photographer in New York was eager to receive the prince and take his picture, but he chose Brady.

The prince presented a rosewood cane to Brady, which he would always cherish. This was another great triumph for Brady of Broadway, who was unquestionably the leading photographer in America.

Despite this success, Brady's world was becoming ever more troubled. The states were bitterly arguing about the future of the Union. Influential Southerners wanted to break off and establish their own nation, and many Northerners were demanding an end to slavery, a system that supported the Southern economy. There was growing risk of armed conflict between North and South. With the nation in turmoil, a presidential election got under way in 1860. Of course, the leading candidates came to Brady for their pictures.

SHADOWS ON THE WALLS

In the 1850s, Broadway resident and poet Caleb Lyon wrote "Stanzas," a poem with the subtitle, "Suggested by a Visit to Brady's Portrait Gallery." It opened with a first impression of the famous Americans pictured on the walls:

> Soul-lit shadows now around me;
> They who armies nobly led;
> They who make a nation's glory
> While they're living—when they're dead,
> Land-marks for our country's future,
> Have their genius left behind;
> Victors from the field of battle;
> Victors from the field of mind . . .

For many people who viewed these portraits in Brady's gallery, the experience was inspiring. Photographs still seemed magical—a kind of alchemy.

> Like a spirit land of shadows
> They in silence on me gaze,
> And I feel my heart is beating
> With the pulse of other days;
> And I ask what great magician
> Conjured forms like these afar?
> Echo answers, 'tis the sunshine,
> By the alchemist Daguerre—

A Likeness of a Future President

The candidate who seemed least likely to win in the coming election was Abraham Lincoln. A little-known Republican from Illinois, Lincoln called for the nation to remain united.

The people of New York City, who were mainly against slavery and were pro-Union, hardly knew Lincoln when he arrived in February 1860. Antislavery editor William Cullen Bryant brought Lincoln to Brady's Tenth Street gallery. Lincoln was travel-weary, tired and worn from the campaign.

Brady found the 6-foot-4 Lincoln difficult to photograph. For one thing, the stand for the immobilizer head clamp was not long enough, and Brady had to put it up on

When young Edward, Prince of Wales, visited New York in 1860, the city's residents welcomed him with great excitement. Edward set aside ceremonial duties to make a special visit to Brady's studio for this full-length portrait.

Brady photographed presidential candidate Abraham Lincoln on February 27, 1860. This image is known as the "Cooper Union portrait" because Lincoln had just given a stirring speech at the school. The portrait was copied as a lithograph and widely published, gaining Lincoln some much-needed publicity.

LINCOLN'S 1860 CAMPAIGN

America's political and social conflicts came to a head with the presidential election of 1860. Four candidates ran for president, each representing a different plan for the nation's future.

A central issue was slavery, which was legal in the Southern states and in several "border states" between North and South. Abraham Lincoln and his Republican Party opposed expanding slavery, while the Democratic Party was divided in two, Northern and Southern. Southern Democrats generally wanted to expand slavery, while Northern Democrats were mostly against doing so. A fourth party, the Constitutional Union Party, wanted to compromise and keep the Union and the Constitution as they were, without change.

Senator Stephen A. Douglas of Illinois was the Northern Democratic candidate. Two years earlier, Douglas had defeated Lincoln in an election for the Senate. In the 1860 presidential campaign, however, Lincoln was elected with 1.86 million votes, while Douglas received 1.38 million votes, the second-highest amount.

Immediately after Lincoln's election, the Southern Democrats reorganized. Starting with South Carolina, Southern states began seceding from the Union. President Lincoln opposed secession, which ultimately led the nation into the Civil War.

Illinois senator Stephen A. Douglas ran unsuccessfully against Abraham Lincoln for president in the campaign of 1860. Photographed at Brady's studio in 1855, Douglas appears in all his flamboyant elegance.

"American Senator Stephen A. Douglas." Mathew B. Brady, c. 1855

a stool. Also, Lincoln's long neck poked out of his shirt collar, which hung too low, and his ribbon necktie was loose.

"I had great trouble in making a natural picture," Brady later recalled. "When I got him before the camera, I asked him if I might not arrange his collar, and with that he began to pull it up."

"Ah," Lincoln said, "I see you want to shorten my neck."

"That's just it," Brady replied, and they both laughed, which made Lincoln more at ease and a better subject.

For all Lincoln's weariness, he had just scored a great personal triumph with a thrilling speech to New York Republicans. They had cheered him wildly for his promise not to accept any state's withdrawal from the Union. Now, thousands of Americans who read newspaper reports about Lincoln's speech wanted to know what he looked like.

Brady's photograph from this session was engraved by the newspapers and published widely. Thousands more copies of the picture were printed and sold around the country. Brady showed Lincoln as a fine-looking, distinguished gentleman instead of the homely, gawky country bumpkin his enemies usually described him to be.

Later that year, Lincoln won the election. He said his victory was in part thanks to that speech in New York, which gained him broad national support—and also thanks to Brady's photograph.

Lincoln sat for Brady several times in the following years, and Brady also photographed him at his 1861 presidential inauguration. The president's wife and three sons also sat for Brady, who was presented with the gift of a chair by Lincoln. This chair had been Lincoln's when he served in the House of Representatives as a member from Illinois. The chair now became a familiar prop in Brady's studio and appeared in many photographs—and always in Lincoln's pictures, of course.

Lincoln's election shook the foundations of the Union. His stand against secession convinced Southerners to act, and they established the Confederate States of America. Lincoln refused to allow the United States to be torn apart and was prepared to fight for the Union. It was too late for the United States to reach a peaceful solution for its future. That future would be decided by a great and bloody civil war.

Photo taken
July 22nd
1861

BRADY
The Photographer
returned from
Bull Run

Weary and dusty and still wearing a long riding coat, called a duster, Brady poses after returning to his studio on July 22, 1861. This was one day after he witnessed the devastating Union defeat at the First Battle of Bull Run, which had been fought near Manassas, Virginia.

CHAPTER SEVEN

A Spirit Said, "Go"

I can only describe the destiny that overruled
me by saying . . . I had to go. A spirit in my
feet said, "Go," and I went.
–Mathew Brady

When the storm of the Civil War finally broke upon the United States in April 1861, Mathew Brady was determined to record it in photographs. As eager Union volunteers put on their new uniforms, Brady's gallery in New York and his gallery under Alexander Gardner in Washington did enormous business in cartes de visite. Soldiers of every rank wanted their pictures taken in uniform and sent to loved ones.

But Brady intended do more than make cartes de visite. He would photograph history, capturing the coming clash just as he had captured the images of what he called "illustrious Americans" in his gallery. Brady planned to go into the field and photograph the march of armies, the campaigns, and the ordinary soldiers. It would be difficult, dangerous, and expensive. (About ten years earlier, photographers had first followed troops into battle during the Crimean War. Their close-up images of British and Russian soldiers' lonely and dangerous lives had stirred viewers around the world.)

Few photographers had the equipment, experience, or funds to follow the conflict in the field. The cost of hiring and supplying a photography crew would be high, even for a short campaign. Brady's galleries were doing great business, however, and money was rolling in. He also expected to profit by selling copies of the war pictures he took.

President Lincoln himself gave Brady an official pass, permitting him to accompany the Union Army. Brady knew most of the important commanders, since they had been patrons of his studios.

BRADY'S WHAT'S-IT WAGON

Mathew Brady designed special wagons for conducting photography in the field. Each was a traveling darkroom and photo-supply closet. Built from a delivery wagon—a small space for photographic facilities by the standards of the day—it was tightly hooded with black cloth that kept out light.

There was a door at the back, with a sturdy step that was boxed in. The photographer could stand there while working with chemicals, glass negatives, and paper set in another box inside the wagon. This work had to be done quickly. Negatives had to be developed immediately, before dust, insects, and heat—or even drops of sweat—damaged them.

The wagon's cabinets and shelves held extra lenses, boxes of glass plates and negatives, cameras, and tripods. A lightproof tent could be set up on the ground as a darkroom when the crew was in camp.

There also had to be room to carry food, bedding, and extra clothes, and a place for men to sleep when no tents could be set up. To Brady and his crews, a "what's-it wagon" meant an everything-wagon.

Brady's teams of photographers and assistants traveled to scenes of battle in specially designed wagons fitted out with cameras and darkroom equipment. Even men hired as the drivers learned the art and craft of photography in the field, where every hand was needed.

A worried Juliette Brady and several friends tried to talk Mathew out of following the army, but they were unsuccessful. Asked years later why he had been so eager to go to the war, Brady said, "I can only describe the destiny that overruled me by saying . . . I had to go. A spirit in my feet said, 'Go,' and I went."

The First Battle

In summer 1861, two military forces gathered near Washington, D.C. One was fighting for the United States, called the Union Army. The other was the Confederate Army, representing the Southern slave states, or Confederate States. Both armies had been quickly organized and were short of training. The soldiers on each side expected to defeat the other easily and with little bloodshed. No one thought the war would last very long—six months at most.

The Union regiments tramped into Virginia in the steamy heat of July 1861, flags flying and drums beating. Thousands of excited civilians in carriages and on horseback went along, intending to picnic and watch the coming battle from a distance.

Wearing a wide-brimmed hat and a full-length riding coat, called a duster, Brady traveled with the invasion force. He had fitted out a special wagon with cabinets and shelves to hold photographic supplies and equipment. The wagon had a black cloth hood to keep out light so the photographer could develop negatives inside. At first, the wagon seemed mysterious to the soldiers. Some thought that it was a hearse to carry the dead from the battlefield. Others called it a "what's-it wagon," a name that stuck.

When Brady's wagon came to an interesting scene, he called a halt, and his crew unloaded the heavy camera with its tripod stand. They photographed several landscapes, a railroad depot, and destroyed bridges. When rain set in, the roads became muddy. Firing was heard in the distance, but Brady's wagon could not get near the action.

Soon, the danger turned out to be far worse than expected. The Union army was defeated, and soldiers came streaming back, many of them wounded. It was time for Brady to get away from the fighting, but his wagon was surrounded by soldiers mingled with fleeing civilian carriages. It was almost impossible to get a wagon through the mass of soldiers and civilians. Brady stopped to take pictures of the crowd pushing along the road to Washington.

The rumble of guns sounded closer, warning of the Confederate Army's approach. Confusion gave way to fear, and fear to panic. Those who were able began to run. Suddenly, the photography wagon was jolted by the frightened mob and shoved aside.

Then it overturned. Supplies and equipment inside crashed and shattered. To

In the summer of 1861, Centerville, Virginia, was a center of conflict between the forces of North and South. Brady staff photographer George N. Barnard framed this Union detachment guarding a bridge.

Brady's dismay, many glass negatives were broken, and the pictures on them were lost. He and his men saved what they could, righted the wagon, and continued their escape under the sound of enemy guns.

Arriving back in Washington, exhausted and dirty, Brady immediately had himself photographed in his straw hat and duster. It was the first of many pictures to remind him of his war experiences.

The War Rages On

The North was humiliated by the defeat, which later became known as the First Battle of Bull Run. It was now obvious that the conflict would last longer than anyone had imagined. One Confederate hero of the battle was Brady's former subject, Thomas J. Jackson, known as "Stonewall" for standing like a "stone wall" in the face of enemy assault.

Brady's photographs of the campaign were displayed at his Washington gallery, and he was widely praised for his efforts. Convinced that he could make a profit by continuing to photograph the war, he prepared to invest whatever was necessary. He engaged courageous and skillful camera operators to form several crews and cover different aspects of the war.

Black-hooded Brady wagons became familiar sights to the soldiers during the next major campaign, fought in eastern Virginia in mid-1862. The wide hat, duster, and the "cross of a mustache and beard" readily identified Brady the photographer.

WAR PHOTOGRAPHERS

The Civil War saw the first appearance of professional war photographers in large numbers. At least 300 independent photographers went into the field. Some became famous names in this early period of American photography: Alexander Gardner and his brother, James, Timothy N. O'Sullivan, Lewis H. Landy, David Knox, T.C. Roche, William R. Pywell, and David B. Woodbury.

Several, like O'Sullivan and Alexander Gardner, left Brady to work for other photographers or to start their own photography businesses. Some of Brady's photographers were African Americans, including A.B. Foons, who drove a wagon and also operated a camera.

The soldiers were glad when photographers were on hand to record a campaign for history. When men were off duty, they often had their pictures taken, usually for a dollar. (A Union soldier's pay was just $13 a month.)

A photographer could profit immensely in camp, taking as many as 150 portraits a day.

"Sergeant Dore, an enlisted man with the 7th New York State Militia." Mathew B. Brady, 1861

This sergeant is a member of the 7th New York State Militia, an elite regiment formed before the Civil War. The regiment was composed of men from prominent northeastern families and was the first to reach Washington, D.C., after war was declared in April 1861.

The Union commander was General George B. McClellan, a friend of Brady's. McClellan allowed him to work freely, even letting camera operators rise above the armies in an observation balloon. This campaign turned out to be yet another disastrous Union defeat, but Lincoln would not give up. The war continued.

Later in 1862, Brady went to the campaigns of Antietam, Maryland, and Fredericksburg, Virginia. Cameramen were kept behind the troops, away from the shooting. Pictures were taken of important bridges and captured towns, usually before or after the battle. When fighting raged, though, bullets and cannonballs flew everywhere and were a danger for miles around the action.

Hot air balloons were used to observe enemy movements behind the lines and often were targets of artillery fire and sharpshooters. This Union Army balloon, the *Intrepid*, is shown operating in eastern Virginia during the 1862 Peninsular Campaign.

The horrors of war were publicly exhibited to civilians in photographs such as this, from the 1862 Battle of Antietam in Maryland. Confederate dead lie near the Dunker Church, the scene of much fierce fighting during the engagement.

Antietam had been a draw, but at Fredericksburg the Union lost again. There, Brady photographed men of the Irish Brigade, who were resting after making an attack. Within a few hours, some of these soldiers would be killed when they returned to battle.

Brady or his crews photographed Union headquarters and encampments, hospitals, artillery positions, and trenches. There were many important places and events they could not get to, such as coastal campaigns, enemy prisoner-of-war camps, or ruined Southern cities. These images were taken by others and purchased for Brady's collection.

Once again, Brady bought and copied other photographers' pictures, usually putting his own name on them. This practice was not uncommon in those days, before strict copyright laws came into effect. Some of the best Civil War pictures, however, were taken by Brady's crews, often with him present. A number of photographs show him standing off to the side, smiling at the camera, and wearing his trademark wide-brimmed hat.

Brady surveys the now-peaceful fields and woods of Gettysburg a day after the great Union victory there in 1863. The photographer wears his trademark wide-brimmed straw hat, which identified him to the soldiers wherever he appeared.

CHAPTER EIGHT

The Eye of History

The camera is the eye of history.
You must never make bad pictures.
—Mathew Brady

In July 1863, Mathew Brady looked over the battlefield at Gettysburg, Pennsylvania. It was now quiet but littered with the destruction of war: shattered cannon, broken wagons, dead horses, and the torn clothing and lost shoes and knapsacks of fallen soldiers.

Gettysburg had been a great Union victory, but the total cost was more than 43,000 Americans killed, wounded, and missing. The victorious Union army had picked up its dead and wounded, but the defeated Confederates had left many dead behind. Photographers found the bodies of Southerners among the trees and rocks, where they had fallen.

In some cases, the photographer placed a rifle at a dead man's side for a more dramatic effect. Bodies often were moved to create a more effective scene for the camera. Some photographs showed bodies scattered in open fields after an attack. Others lay in rows, ready for burial.

By the time battlefield pictures went on display in Northern cities, the engagement they recorded had become famous. Many people could not bear to attend these exhibits. The sorrows of war were too much for them. Even book and newspaper publishers did not use Brady's images of the dead.

"These are terrible mementoes," wrote Massachusetts poet Oliver Wendell Holmes, after viewing Brady's pictures of fallen soldiers. "Let him who wishes to know what war is, look at these."

The proud Confederate army was in retreat from Gettysburg in 1863 when Alexander Gardner photographed this fallen Southern infantryman. It is believed that this body was moved and the rifle placed in clear view before the picture was taken.

Under Fire

In 1864, Brady journeyed to northern Virginia to photograph General Ulysses S. Grant and his staff in the field. Brady had already taken Grant's portrait when the general first arrived in Washington, D.C., to assume command of Union forces.

Opposite: Brady photographed Union commander General Ulysses S. Grant at field headquarters during the final Virginia campaign of 1865. Brady's other photographs of Grant's headquarters revealed an efficient group of veteran officers who trusted their general.

Month after month, Grant's army slowly pushed back the Confederates under General Robert E. Lee. As they followed this campaign, Brady and his crew sometimes came under fire. In one instance, a Union artillery battery posed for his camera, with Brady standing in the midst of it all. The men went through the drill of loading and aiming, and their activity stirred up Confederate gunners, who expected a bombardment and began to fire.

Shells exploded all around, knocking down the camera. When the firing stopped, Brady found the camera was undamaged. He set it up again and continued photographing the artillerymen before renewed Confederate firing forced his crew to take cover.

Brady spent more than $100,000 photographing the conflict, financing photography crews, and buying other photographers' pictures. He received little financial return from his war pictures, so, in order to raise funds, he sold his real estate and stocks. As his business situation worsened, he too often neglected paying his creditors, including some of his staff photographers. By 1865, Brady's personal wealth had been drastically reduced. Still, he kept on buying pictures for his Civil War collection.

The Face of the Confederacy

At last, the Union's superior power and Grant's relentless attacks forced Lee to surrender at Appomattox, Virginia, on April 9, 1865. The Confederacy was defeated, and the war came to a close. Just days after Lee's surrender, Brady visited the general's Virginia home. There, Lee gallantly put on his uniform for a portrait. It is a testament to Brady's high reputation that he could persuade the sorrowful Lee to pose for him. "There was little conversation during the sitting," Brady later said, "but the General changed his position as often as I wished him to."

Until then, the world had seen only an 1851 daguerreotype of Lee in their newspapers. With Brady's portrait, everyone finally saw the face of the Confederacy's greatest and most-loved commander. Even in defeat, Lee appeared noble and proud, thanks to the abilities of Mathew Brady.

Brady and Lee did not know it at the time, but President Lincoln had just been assassinated. Brady was soon back in Washington for the unhappy task of photographing his friend's funeral procession.

Unwanted Pictures

The Civil War had lasted four years, with twenty-nine major campaigns, seventy-six battles, and more than 10,000 military actions. Brady accumulated at least 7,000 pictures of people and places during the war.

Just days after the Confederacy's utter defeat in April 1865, Confederate commanding general Robert E. Lee was willing to pose for the highly respected Mathew Brady. The war-weary Lee was photographed at his home in Arlington, Virginia.

He soon found that no one wanted them. In the first years after the Civil War, not even the federal government was interested in Brady's photographs, even though it was an important pictorial record. Most Americans wanted to forget the terrible conflict, to put it behind them forever.

Brady's financial troubles were made worse by a national depression and other business difficulties. His debts mounted, and legal actions were brought against him for payment. As a result, he began losing nearly all he owned. He tried again and again to convince the government to purchase his collection of Civil War and other photographs. Congress agreed that the images were important but did not agree with Brady's estimate that his pictures were worth $100,000.

"I have spent a lifetime collecting the works I now offer," he said. "I have kept an open gallery at the Capital of the Nation for more than a quarter of a century to assist in obtaining historical portraits, and have spent time and money enough, dictated by pride and patriotism."

The press and many government officials agreed that Brady's pictures were "great historical works of art." They urged Congress to acquire them "and place them in the Capital, where all the world can study the progress of the Civil War in pages copied from life itself."

In 1874, the owner of the New York warehouse where thousands of Brady's negatives were stored demanded that the back rent be paid. When Brady could not pay, the negatives were auctioned off for $1,800. The buyer promptly sold them to the federal government for $2,500. Brady received nothing.

A year later, former Union general and now Congressman John Garfield of Ohio rose to give a speech in Congress, criticizing the government for taking advantage of Brady's financial distress. (Garfield had once sat for Brady.) "I know something of the tremendous difficulties of securing them," Garfield said, recalling his years as a wartime commander.

Garfield finally convinced Congress to appropriate $25,000 to pay Brady for all rights to those negatives. It was a triumph, but after paying off his most pressing debts, there was little left for Brady.

Last Years

Brady continued to work at small studios he ran in Washington and New York. He was most famous for having photographed so many presidents, and it became a tradition that he should take the portrait of each new president. They all considered it an honor to sit for Brady immediately after their inaugurations.

In the early 1880s, Juliette Brady fell seriously ill with a heart condition. Mathew's own health also worsened. He was almost blind and suffered from a kidney ailment as well as from bouts of rheumatism. When Juliette died in 1887, he was heartbroken.

Debts continued to plague Brady, who had to close his New York gallery. He moved his Washington gallery several times after 1889, always to a less costly space. Yet he had friends and admirers who respected all that he had achieved.

In 1891, *World* reporter George A. Townsend unexpectedly dropped in on Brady's modest Washington studio. Townsend found a "trim, wiry, square-shouldered figure with the light of an Irish sun-shower in his smile." Brady was wearing his blue-tinted spectacles as the two of them spoke about the legendary photographer's fifty-year career. Townsend wrote that it was thanks to the dedication of Mathew B. Brady that "We possess many a face in the pencil of the sun."

Mathew Brady's Legacy

Although Brady could barely see by the early 1890s, he began working on a slide show of his wartime pictures. Famous generals agreed to make remarks at the presentation, scheduled for early 1896.

Then, while crossing a Washington street in December 1895, Brady was run over by a horse cart and his leg was broken. He moved back to New York to recover from his injury, but his ill health had weakened him. A few weeks later, Brady collapsed, suffering from severe kidney problems. He died in the hospital on January 15, 1896, at (about) age seventy-two.

The obituary in Washington's *Evening Star* newspaper best expressed what Mathew Brady meant to his country: "News of his passing will be received with sincere sorrow by hundreds and hundreds who knew this gentle photographer, whose name is today a household word all over the United States."

Friends took up a collection to arrange for burial in the Congressional Cemetery in Washington, a place of the highest honor. There, Brady lies beside many of the notables he had photographed during his career. (As with Brady's uncertain date of birth, the wrong year—1895—was mistakenly engraved on his tombstone.)

Since Mathew Brady's time, every illustrated history of the Civil War has included his images. Brady's belief that his photographs composed a unique and valuable historical collection has proven to be true. The Library of Congress holds most of Brady's photographs, which are essential for Americans, past and future, who want to know about this chapter in the story of their country.

"The camera is the eye of history," Mathew Brady once said. "You must never make bad pictures."

GLOSSARY

Camera—A device for making photographs by allowing light into a chamber and exposing a surface coated with light-sensitive chemicals.

Camera obscura—A Latin term meaning "dark chamber" and referring to the earliest cameras. When light enters the darkened chamber through a tiny pinhole opening, the beam projects an image of the outside scene onto a surface.

Carte-de-visite—A French term for a small photographic portrait, which was widely used as a personal calling card in the 1860s.

Daguerreotype—An early photograph developed on a silver-plated metal sheet treated with light-sensitive chemicals. Daguerreotypy was the first form of photography, invented by Louis Daguerre in France.

Daguerreotype artist—An expert daguerreotypist who usually managed a studio, posed the subject, prepared the lighting, and directed the taking of the picture by a camera operator.

Darkroom—A lightproof area for preparing photographic plates and processing negatives and for printing photographs. A darkroom is also used for loading and unloading some cameras.

Engraving—A picture created by cutting, or engraving, lines onto special wooden blocks, stone tablets, or metal plates that are then coated with ink and pressed against paper to make a printed image.

Exposure—The length of time light is allowed to act on a photographic material.

Immobilizer—A clamp on a floor stand in a photographic studio to hold a person in place.

Lens—An optical glass or similar material that collects and focuses rays of light to form a sharp image inside a camera.

Lithograph—A printed image made from a picture composed of many small lines engraved on special stone tablets; these tablets, or "lithos," are inked and used to print the lithograph.

Miniature cases—Sometimes called "snap cases," these held painted miniatures and photographs; they were fastened with hooks or clasps and came in various styles. The image was sealed with glass and inserted into a thin brass outer frame to hold it in place.

Negative—An image in which the highlights and tones are the reverse of the actual subject. Transparent glass or film negatives are used to make a positive photographic print.

"Pencil of the Sun"—A term for the first photographs, known as daguerreotypes.

Photography—The art or process of producing images—photographs—on photosensitive surfaces. Photographic images usually are made on paper, but they can be made on any surface that can be coated with a light-sensitive material, including cloth, canvas, ivory, and tin.

Photosensitive—Being sensitive to radiant energy, such as light. Photosensitive chemicals darken when exposed to light.

Print—A photographic image created on light-sensitive paper by exposing the paper to light through a negative.

Stereograph—Two identical images, which when viewed simultaneously by both eyes give the impression of depth, or three dimensions.

Tintype—A photographic method of the mid-nineteenth century, which used a light-sensitive coating applied on a thin metal plate. Tintypes were not made of tin, however, but of iron.

TIME LINE

1823 or 1824: Mathew B. Brady is born in Warren County, New York.

1835: Brady travels to Albany, New York, for treatment of inflammation of his eyes. He leaves home to work as assistant to portrait artist William Page.

1839: Brady arrives in New York City where he meets Samuel F.B. Morse and learns to make daguerreotypes. Brady manufactures portrait and jewelry cases and works in a store while studying with Morse.

1844: Brady opens Brady's Daguerrean Miniature Gallery, in New York City on Broadway, at Fulton Street.

1845: He exhibits portraits of famous Americans.

1849: He opens a studio in Washington, D.C., and makes portraits of many politicians.

1850: Brady's *Gallery of Illustrious Americans* is published.

1850 or 1851: Brady marries Juliette Handy.

1851: Brady's daguerreotypes win a medal at the Crystal Palace Exhibition in London.

1853: He opens a new studio at 359 Broadway in New York City.

1856: Brady exhibits Brady Imperials, large portrait photographs printed on canvas and hand-colored with oil paint.

1858: Brady's National Photographic Art Gallery opens in Washington, D.C.

1859: He opens a new studio in New York City at 643 Bleecker Street, at the corner of Broadway.

1860: Brady opens his fourth and last New York City studio, the National Portrait Gallery, at 785 Broadway.

1861–1865: Civil War between the North and the South engulfs the nation.

1861: Brady makes an inaugural portrait of Abraham Lincoln in his Washington, D.C., portrait studio. He attempts to photograph the First Battle of Bull Run near Manassas, Virginia.

1862: Brady exhibits his associate Alexander Gardner's photographs of the Battle of Antietam.

1864: Brady photographs Union General Ulysses S. Grant on campaign in Virginia.

1865: Brady photographs Confederate commander Robert E. Lee just days after Lee's surrender at Appomattox. Brady also photographs Lincoln's funeral procession.

1868: Brady's financial troubles grow worse. He opens a new Washington, D.C., studio on Pennsylvania Avenue.

1873: Brady files for bankruptcy.

1875: Congress pays $25,000 for the ownership of Brady's collection of negatives and prints.

1887: Juliette Handy Brady dies.

1895: Brady is struck by a horse cart in Washington and breaks a leg. He prepares for an illustrated lecture based on his Civil War photographs. He moves back to New York City to recover from his injuries.

1896: Mathew Brady dies on January 15, in New York City. He is buried in the Congressional Cemetery, in Washington, D.C.

FURTHER RESEARCH

ABOUT MATHEW BRADY

Hobart, George. *Mathew Brady*. London: Macdonald, 1984.
Meredith, Roy. *Mathew Brady's Portrait of an Era*. New York: W.W. Norton, 1982.
Milhollen, Hirst D. "The Mathew B. Brady Collection." In *A Century of Photographs, 1846–1946*. Washington, DC: Library of Congress, 1980, 30–37.

National Portrait Gallery, Smithsonian Institution
"Mathew Brady's National Portrait Gallery: A Virtual Tour"
www.npg.si.edu/exh/brady/gallery/bradindx.html

Old Picture.com
"Mathew Brady Studio"
www.old-picture.com/mathew-brady-studio-index-003.htm

ABOUT THE CIVIL WAR

Ketchum, Richard M., ed. *The Civil War*. New York: American Heritage, 1960.
Murray, Aaron R., ed. *Civil War Battles and Leaders*. New York: DK Publishing, 2004.

The American Civil War
sunsite.utk.edu/civil-war

CivilWar.com
www.civilwar.com

The Civil War Home Page
www.rugreview.com/cw/cwhp.htm

"Selected Civil War Photographs." Library of Congress, American Memory
memory.loc.gov/ammem/cwphtml/cwphome.html

The United States Civil War
www.us-civilwar.com

ABOUT PHOTOGRAPHY

Metropolitan Museum of Art
The Daguerreian Era and Early American Photography in History: 1839–1860
www.metmuseum.org/TOAH/HD/adag/hd_adag.htm

The Star Camera Company
www.geocities.com/starcameracompany/index2.htm

University of Southern California
Lost and Found: A Case for Early Photography
imsc.usc.edu/haptics/LostandFound/terms_case.html

BIBLIOGRAPHY

BOOKS AND ARTICLES

Cobb, Josephine. "Photographers of the Civil War." *Military Affairs,* 26:3, Autumn 1962, 127–135.

Hoobler, Dorothy, and Thomas Hoobler. *Photographing History: The Career of Mathew Brady.* New York: G.P. Putnam, 1977.

Horan, James D. *Mathew Brady: Historian with a Camera.* New York: Bonanza, 1955.

Kunhardt, Dorothy Meserve, Philip B. Kunhardt, and Editors of Time-Life Books. *Mathew Brady and His World.* Alexandria, VA: Time-Life Books, 1977.

WEB SITES

National Portrait Gallery, Smithsonian Institution
"Mathew Brady's Portraits."
www.npg.si.edu/exh/brady/index2.htm

National Portrait Gallery
"Mathew Brady's World."
www.npg.si.edu/exh/brady/intro/cont4.htm

SOURCE NOTE

Direct quotations by Mathew Brady in this book are taken from the books about him by James D. Horan, Dorothy Meserve Kunhardt and Philip B. Kunhardt, and Roy Meredith. These books are out of print but may be found in the library. The best online resource for seeing Brady images is the Smithsonian's National Portrait Gallery, which is listed first among the Web sites. This site has both biographical and photographic information about Mathew Brady and his time.

INDEX

ABOUT THE AUTHOR

Stuart A. P. Murray has written many books, both fiction and nonfiction, for young readers. Among his many works about the history of war are *Witness to the Civil War,* a revision of the 1895 *Leslie's Illustrated History of the Civil War, Civil War Battles & Leaders,* and *A Time of War,* which traces the role of Massachusetts in the American Civil War. In his long years of interest in the Civil War, Murray has found Mathew Brady's photographs to provide an unsurpassed close-up view of the people and places of this era of crisis in the United States. Murray lives in Petersburgh, New York.

PICTURE CREDITS